My Cup is Full

The Poetic Journey of an Ordinary Woman
(With a Playful Imagination)

Lisa Louise Fuller

Visit our website at
www.StillwaterPress.com
for more information.

First Stillwater River Publications Edition.

ISBN: 978-1-963296-90-7

1 2 3 4 5 6 7 8 9 10
Written by Lisa Louise Fuller.
Cover photograph by Ruth Black / Adobe Stock.
Cover & interior book design by Matthew St. Jean.
Published by Stillwater River Publications,
West Warwick, RI, USA.

Names: Fuller, Lisa Louise, author.
Title: My cup is full : the poetic journey of an ordinary
woman (with a playful imagination) / Lisa Louise Fuller.
Description: First Stillwater River Publications edition. |
West Warwick, RI, USA : Stillwater River Publications, [2024]
Identifiers: ISBN: 978-1-963296-90-7
Subjects: LCSH: Holism—Poetry. | Healing—Poetry. |
Loneliness—Poetry. | Inspiration—Poetry. | Grief—Poetry. |
Joy—Poetry. | LCGFT: Poetry.
Classification: LCC: PS3606.U555 M9 2024 |
DDC: 811/.6—dc23

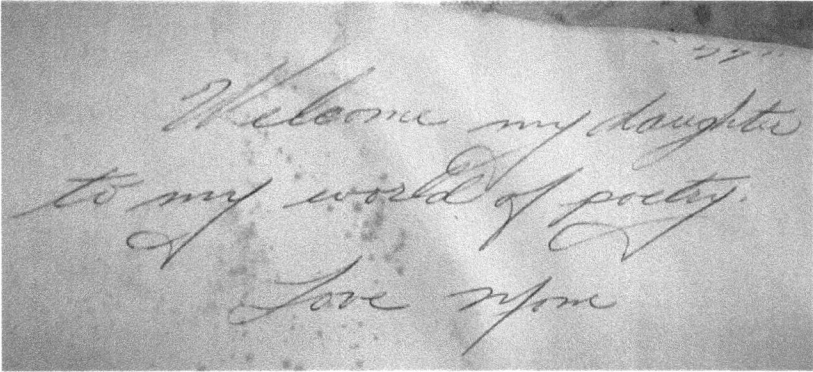

Welcome my daughter
to my world of poetry.
Love Mom

❀

This book is dedicated to my beautiful mother, Eleanor Gregson,
who filled my heart with immense love and my imagination
with fairy tales and poetry.
I love you, mom, "toujours"

❀

My Cup is Full

"As for the usefulness of poetry, its uses are many.
It is the deification of reality. It should make our days holy to us.
The poet should speak to all men, for a moment, of that other life
of theirs that they have smothered and forgotten."

Dame Edith Sitwell
(1887 – 1964)

Contents

Preface

❧

In my humble opinion, we need poetry more than ever before. We need enchantment and to stop smothering it away. And we need to allow ourselves this outlet to express our emotions in a healthy way. This can only be done by the avenues of the heart. We need to feel them in their fullest capacity to bring us ever closer to our greatest level of understanding of all the magic that life has to offer. It is a hunger within all of us longing to be satisfied, not only for our human self, but our higher self; that divine, God-given heart and soul, for we are all co-creators with the Universe.

Our deepest roots – our desires and emotions – are not dissimilar to the roots of the magnificent trees. We need to remember we are all connected in this "oneness" to Mother Earth, and as we allow ourselves to open to her beauty, as well as our own, we give permission for our emotional vulnerability to humbly blossom like the branches of the trees. In those moments we shine brightly in our true authenticity for all to cherish and for God. That, I believe, is to truly live an enchanted life.

Introduction

It has taken me many years to finally put this book together - years of procrastination and doubt because, for me, my poetry is very personal. I have been writing poems since I was very young. I remember the day my mother gave me my first 8 ½ x 11 journal. I began to take all the poems I had written until then and pen them in, one by one. Now, at 60 years old, each one shares deeply in the story of my life, but I also believe it tells the story of the lives of many women – all the pain, love, loneliness, discoveries, sorrows, and joys we all have experienced at one time or another, all very personal to each of us, uniquely. I can read each poem, prose, or inspirational quote and know exactly how I was feeling and what I was going through like it was as fresh as the day I experienced it. So, although I did not keep a diary all my life, these journals read like the autobiography of my life – a life of an ordinary woman (with a playful imagination).

I invite you to travel through the pages of this book with me. I hope it inspires you and blesses your life with a little enchantment and kinship.

So, from my heart to yours, I give you *My Cup is Full*. Indeed, it truly is!

"With the love of the angels in your heart, Heaven's wind in your soul, and Mother Earth's guidance at your feet."
Lisa Louise Fuller

And so began my life as a poet...

❧

The year I began penning my poetry in my first journal was 1977, and one of the poems I wrote was for my mother called *Someday*. How completely appropriate to begin this book because she was not only my mother; she was also my best friend. And although I am grateful to say she is still with us, sadly a brain tumor that the doctors removed in 2020 has taken a part of her that was never able to return. It was also the beginning of the Covid lockdowns. It was a devasting, difficult time for my family. I know I'm not the only one who endured such hardships and heartache during that time.

Don't wait till "someday" to tell her that you love her. You just never know when it will be the last.

Someday

Someday when my mother says "good night" to me,

I'll tell her that I love her.

Maybe tomorrow, or the next day.

I always seem to forget to say,

those few mere words that mean so much.

She knows I love her,

because I express it in many other ways.

Someday when my mother says "good morning" to me,

I'll tell her that I love her,

and then she'll smile because we're so close.

But I always seem to forget.

Someday I'll leave her,

and the good night and good morning stage in our home,

will be empty,

because I always seem to forget.

But someday is today,

because smiles shouldn't only have to come on special occasions,

especially when they're so meaningful to say.

"Mother dear, I love you!"

February 16, 1979

The Old Oak Tree

Every day I pass by the old oak tree,
and read the initials carved just to see,
if my initials were carved with yours.
But my initials were never there,
my favorite spot was empty and bare,
so I'd pass by and leave behind,
the old oak tree.
Then one day I was passing by,
I saw your face and caught your eye.
Your finger pointed to the old oak tree,
and in my favorite spot I could clearly see,
the initials for you and me.
As days go by the tree grows older,
the night winds cry, and the world grows colder,
but our initials you will always see,
in the old oak tree.

March 5, 1978

To A Lost Summer Love

Yesterday, he came.
Now I shall live forever with shoulder's untouched,
and love thrown aside.
All too soon you came, but the exit was clear,
leaving me like the ebb of the tide.
Today, and every day, and my moments,
counting the hours and the days that went.
I shall never forget the day we met,
the soft, brown hair with a smile that was only lent.
Now you hurt me, but you don't know, and you probably won't.
Like the thorn of a rose causing me to bleed
only my heart is turning from red to blue,
making me feel like a peasant, not a queen.
The soft, lush sand so cold yet so warm with you beside me,
and now I morn, for what was today is yesterday,
and not even teardrops can take your place.
Gone in the wind, a lost summer love.
A desolate silhouette wanders astray in the moonlight,
searching for a lost summer love whose far away.

August 1977
Summer at my meme's beach house at Point Judith
My first broken heart

Emptiness

Emptiness is not being alone, but to be alone,
when there are many people in a room, yet you're lonely.
Emptiness is something that was for keepsake,
and suddenly taken away from you.
Like a slap in the face, you're the dirt under a person's shoe,
and it hurts.
Emptiness is a misfit, talking to someone and feeling ignored.
Emptiness is bitter.
It's the wintry cold that never left but settled in your heart,
and was left bare.
Emptiness is a wall that no person can knock down,
a lonely person buried in the dry, hot sand.
Emptiness is the mask of makeup that lets no one see,
the tears or the pain that never ceases to leave your eyes,
and yet you can see the emptiness no one cares to notice.
No one to find the woman who slowly sank down to a hurting child.
Emptiness is the opposite of happiness,
that someone has taken away,
and as it travels farther into the distance, your mind asks you –
will it ever come back?

January 12, 1979

A Woman

A dash of elegance, a trifle of worry,
a word of regret, and to say I'm sorry.
With an air, conceited, or modest yet bold,
a touch of finesse, and a soft hand to hold.
Evening eyes full of warmth, a day spent like a child,
over-sensitive tears, a voice powerful yet mild.
A comical laugh, a heart full of gold,
a wish to dream about, and a baby to hold.
A fickle little puzzle, but a world of fantasy,
new pieces to explore, but never to solve the mystery.
A fragrance of beauty, a locket of hair in a bow,
walking two inches taller, and for others bending low.
Tender as a rose, as brilliant as the radiant sun,
a burst of ambition and having such fun!
Taking life in stride, keeping memories in a chest,
forgiving all the bad times and reliving the best.
A mother, a daughter, a little girl at heart,
and always a woman, a work of art.

March 29, 1979

I Have Dreams of Being with Someone

I have dreams of being with someone, for no particular reason.
Just to talk or share a moment of inspiration,
for no particular reason,
just... to walk together.
I have dreams of being with someone,
to fill the corner of my mind with a touch,
a hand to encircle warmth in my heart,
for no particular reason, but it can mean so much.
I have dreams of being with someone, for no particular reason.
When boredom is overwhelming,
and the window I gaze out of is just dismal and barren,
till you're with someone and the window beholds
an imaginative world to see!
I have dreams of being with someone, for no particular reason,
except because... I'm lonely, and just outside my window,
there's just... me.

1979

I Want

I want to walk in the rain and smell the dewy air.
I'd like to sleep in a meadow with daisies in my hair.
I want the bluebirds to wake me at the crack of dawn,
I'd like to hold a baby squirrel and breathe in a freshly mowed lawn.
I want to float on my back over wave crests on the sea,
I'd like to make believe I'm an artist and pretend to be painting me.
I want to pop some pink bubble gum and peel it off my face,
I'd like to wrinkle my feet in a stream and hide away
in a secret place.
I want to climb a snow-peaked mountain and roar like a lion,
I'd like to pretend I'm a movie star in a scene where I'm dying.
I want to eat lots of pickles, sour, sweet, and green,
I'd like to pretend I'm a beautiful woman and be treated
like a queen.
I want to carve my initials on a turtle's back,
I'd like to snooze beside a fireplace in the warmth of a sack.
I want to feel the summer breezes weave through my hair,
and as I reach out my hand, I want you always to be there.

June 7, 1979
Published in Teen Magazine, *May 1981*

The Mind Reader

...And as the mind reader gazed within my eyes,
he saw a teardrop that lives within me and hides.
The mind reader looked through me, a pair of lips turned down,
he saw a young man, who had left what he had found.
How little he thought, how much he had,
and the mind reader was stunned and said, "you are so sad!"
The mind reader held my finger, that was marked with time,
and noticed the ring, a vow once shared sublime.
The turning point came when I caught his eye,
and I unburied a misery, that lived deep inside.
...And as the minder reader gazed within my eyes,
I saw a tear that lived within him,
and hides.

1979

A Special Friend

It's always a pleasure to discover in life,
a bright moment in all the blue,
to find a darkened corner
joined together in a silhouette of two.
When all the world has buried you in
your dutiful chores each day,
the hole in which they buried you by becomes
a sandbox, for two, to play.
And when the sea waves pound against your mind,
entangling your worldly dreams,
you find someone who takes you back
to strawberry fields and streams.
That's the very delightful reason,
the reason why special friends are here,
so don't ever fret, nor worry,
because A true friend will always stay near.

December 1979
Dedicated to Allison Cote

There Isn't

There isn't one place that you could bring me,
that I would be more content in,
than your heart.
There isn't one moment you could spare me,
than just one precious second of your time.
There isn't one person,
whom I can see,
the way I see you.
For only a heart is the warmest of places,
and only you can take me there.
For your time to me is so precious,
and yet so few,
and still, I find we can share,
as much as I'd ever hoped to.
And for the way I see you...
it's a face, uncaptured.
It's for the knowing of the character
upon the face of you
that I love.

December 1979

My Failures, How Sore

My failures, how sore, they're a burden to me,
They're the weight upon my shoulders that won't leave me be.
They lengthen my sentence, to weary my woes,
they bring on more troubles that nobody knows.
My failures, how sore, they've imprisoned me,
in all my bitterness that I'm trying to conceive.
They're a plague deep inside me, with seemingly never a cure,
reaching for my happiness, wanting laughter to spur.
As I wear fake sunshine, with a smile on my face,
there's the loneliest stranger that has taken my place.
My failures, how sore, I'm the doer doing no wrong,
but I remain the outcast member, who doesn't belong.
If no laughter will flow, from my river of age,
this as I pen is a desolate page,
for of never to know a second person, no whimsical soul,
no friend enjoys the bitter ice, as it's left out in the cold.
My failures, how sore, but never having to fail,
it's just that this is my road, and it's a dismal trail.

December 4, 1979

When A Stranger Called

As long as I don't speak, I won't cry.
As long as I no longer see your face,
I won't wonder why.
If your absence just leaves me forgetting you,
then let that be.
I don't want to love someone,
whom I am never able to see.
As long as I don't listen to the telephone,
only remembrance will be recalled,
whenever my laughter deserts me,
I just remember when a stranger called.

May 29, 1980

Losing Sight

To not have known you was
a wonderful pleasure,
to daydream from inside of only myself,
anytime.
Whereas, to set my dream free,
the image becomes empty,
and somebody else took that person's place.
Because now I know you,
though it was a wonderful pleasure,
I like dreaming of that
imaginary lover,
whom I never would have lost
like you.

November 1980

Christmas

It's Jack Frost at dawn, the pine trees, ever green,
it's a snowman on a lawn, and Santa Claus in a child's dreams.
It's waking at daylight with Christmas cheer,
it's seeing the wonderous sight of a gift given with thought and care.
It's the carolers' carols, the eggnog and rum,
it's the meaning it holds when Christmas comes.
It's the Manger under radiant lights, it's the Holy birthday,
it's the snowball fights and a one-horse-open-sleigh.
It's a family reunited and a new year ahead,
it's the candle you lit and a prayer to be said.
It's all of which is merry, and a giving gratitude,
it's cheeks red as a berry and a blessing of food.
It's silent and holy, its mistletoe,
it's a celebration of the world and me,
it's our way to show –
our thanks to sweet Jesus, Merry Christmas to you,
as white snowflakes cover over us out from the Heavens of blue.

December 1, 1979
Published in The Lance *college newspaper December 1983*

A Best Friend

You were my best friend.
I slept tucked under your chin every night.
You slipped me under the quilted covers when you had
to sleep with the light.
I always attended your tea parties, once, our picture was snapped,
and when your tooth was pulled you held me tightly upon your lap.
You'd rock me in your rocking chair, and we'd laugh
the hours away,
you drew a crayon-colored picture of me and never threw it away.
But I didn't realize while we were laughing,
how the rocking chair grew smaller for you,
and how the years quickly sped by, our time became
precious and few.
And as the time grew shorter, I was left staring at your closet door,
ever since that day, I didn't see you anymore.
But if you peek inside your closet,
you'll find me waiting there.
Whenever you need some love to hold,
remember, I'm your teddy bear.

October 27, 1983
Published July, 1985 in the American Collegiate Poetry Book
Honorable Mention Award

"The life I want to lead,
was it once here...
in another stage of time?
Someone planted a seed,
as they shed a tear."

1978

And it is Life that I Love

And it is life that I love...
I pretend that each time I draw a deep breath and
wrap my arms around myself,
I place all the beauty of life within.
Like a magnificent person, it stands close to me,
as I caress all it contains in my mind,
And I hold it there, only to have to let it go,
like a swing traveling to and fro I will breathe it in,
hold it, and release it,
knowing that these minutes are some of my favorite
moments of life.
The gifts so freely given by God,
for all to embrace and never take for granted,
whatever one thinks these gifts may be,
cherish them with all your senses and believe –
in miracles, in timelessness, and the human spirit.

July 28, 2000
Track from Via Poetica *CD*

Loneliness

If loneliness had a face, a body, a voice,
we'd be best friends.
Somewhere I've misplaced myself,
like a set of keys or a pair of glasses.
I can't see my way through the darkness
that surrounds me.
Isn't it strange how loneliness seems to know how to
guide me?
This uninvited friend knows all my thoughts,
yet it isn't evil in essence, it's the presence of fear.
I pray that someday soon I will say
goodbye to this friend,
and cast out a net onto warmer waters.
There awaits a new friend
filled with light, hope, and happiness.

October 3, 2002

Somedays, I Smile

Somedays, I smile.
And somedays, when I'm feeling blue,
I imagine that all those raindrops
gently falling outside my window,
are the teardrops shed by the human heart.
Gathered into the loving hands of the angels,
they puddle to the earth,
and dancing above each little pond
are the beautiful fairies,
beaming their delicate rays of
hope and love into the world.
And on those days, I smile.

October 4, 2002
Track from Via Poetica *CD*

*T*he woman sat for hours beside her husband's grave with tears streaming down her face. Her love was nowhere to be seen, to be touched, to be felt or heard. Her heart ached as she placed a white feather near his stone. And as she sighed, she saw a beautiful angel with enormous wings appear in front of her. The angel gently wiped away the teardrops from her cheeks with a soft smile. As she looked deeply into the woman's sad eyes, she sent all the love her husband still felt in his heart for her. The woman could feel it pouring into her body and she soaked it all in with gratitude. Her face began to take on a loving glow!

"How is this possible?!" she asked. The beautiful angel's delicate pink lips said this... "You take it with you, wherever you go. Dear child of God, it never dies. It lives on in your heart and soul!"

The woman let out a soft sigh and smiled. "Mine too?" she asked. "Does he still feel all my love? I miss him so very much."

"Yes. He is beside you always."

It was a beautiful moment, one that she wished she could bottle like the enchanting scent of perfume to wear when the sorrow became too much. She closed her eyes to breathe it all in. When she opened them to say "thank you" the angel had vanished. She began to walk back to her car, opened the door, and there sitting on the passenger seat was a beautiful, white feather. She gently whispered into the air, "Let's go home, my love."

August 29, 2017

He is My Love

He is my love.
No matter where he is, I see him.
He surrounds me with –
his words,
his smile,
his laughter.
He is remembered.
He is waiting for me,
and I will be with him.
But for now, I will love him in return with –
my dreams,
my thoughts, and
my memories of yesteryear.
They will never be lost.
Just kept safely placed in my heart.

October 4, 2002
Dedicated to "Uncle Moe"
Your Cheshire Cat Smile will
always be remembered

Second Half

Now I shall begin the second half of my life with
wisdom, grace, and patience.
The if only's must go, for they serve no purpose in my life.
I shall listen with both my God given ears,
and not just with my eyes for we all wear a different shoe.
I will bend beyond my limit,
like a Willow in a mighty storm,
and lend a helping hand, just because,
and only because I can, I will.
And life on earth will be a better place
because this half of my life, I'm learning that it's only love
the world needs to be Heaven on earth.
I will bring peace to my days, light to my nights,
and surround all around me with
unconditional love and affection.
And my heart will soar to new heights,
and my soul will rejoice in happiness.
For this half of my life, whether it be rich or poor,
will be a fulfilled life because I choose to be blessed by God.

November 22, 2002
Track from Via Poetica *CD*

As I Danced

As I danced with my shadow in the moonlight,
and the trees swayed and played their imaginary violins,
my heart felt as if it would burst!
And I felt no loneliness in life because
I knew that the angels were surrounding me
with love and guidance.
And I didn't feel afraid, for the light of love
was too blindingly bright to notice any fears
trying to sneak upon me with tears of sadness.
For I was one with the Universe,
If just for that moment of time.
Every rock, every tree, and every star
smiled at me as if to say –
"Welcome to our peaceful world. Stay close,
stay in the moment, stay in the light,
forever."

January 7, 2003
Track from Via Poetica *CD*

"Use simple words that speak volumes, for complicated chatter has never managed to sink into the hearts and souls of many. But the simplest and yet deeply felt words of I love you can sink faster than the Titanic to the inner ocean floors of our hearts."

"Treat your home as special and as exciting as you once felt about the tree houses and forts you built during your youth, taking joy and comfort in the fact that you will be dry if it should rain, and all your whispered secrets will remain within those four walls. It is not just a home; it is your sanctuary."

"Take a moment to pretend! Dance as carefree as the ballerina music box dancer you once gazed upon on your bureau, swirling 'round and 'round like an autumn leaf cascading slowly to its winter bed. Imagination is a dying art, yet it is an art we are all quite gifted in."

May 2003

My Christmas Wish

I have a Christmas wish that tugs at my heartstrings,
and brings tears to my eyes,
and no one can fulfill it but you.
And since you are the only one who can
make my wish come true,
I'm asking for you to do this for me –
grant my Christmas wish.
Because I miss you, I dream about you,
and you aren't so angry or unhappy.
You're just you, and I'm just me.
And in my dreams, we walk and talk, and smile at one another,
but, most of all, we are together, just like old times.
So here's my Christmas wish, that no one can fulfill but you.
It doesn't need to be wrapped with a fancy ribbon or bow,
just delivered quietly to my home so I can embrace it,
and say what I've longed to say, face to face, for too long now.
Just three simple words... I love you.
I need say nothing more because that, to me, says it all.

November 17, 2003
Dedicated to Mark

My Magical Snow Globe

My magical snow globe lets me see and feel
your love for one another at Christmastime.
All I need do is gently shake the delicate flakes,
and I'm whisked away to where the two of you are.
Like reading a romantic novel,
all the special emotions you feel for one another
shower down upon me,
and I am filled with happiness for the both of you.
Such an exciting chapter in your lives,
a book with many chapters, I hope,
that never ends –
my favorite book of all.
The world needs snow globes that shower us with love,
and the world needs people like you
to fill us with hope, promise, and joy.
May your Christmas together remain nestled in a part of time
that can be enjoyed every Christmas,
over and over again.

November 29, 2003

Oh, Come to My Dreams

Oh, come to my dreams tonight, dear fairies,
for winter has been too long and white.
Let's laugh, dance, and sing, dear fairies,
under moonbeams of candlelight.
We'll dine on fancy cakes, dear fairies,
and sip on Chamomile tea,
and all my mistakes of yesterday's woes
will float far away from me,
on little carpets of rose petals, dear fairies,
and umbrellas from pistons of flowers.
We'll fly above the treetops, dear fairies,
and gaze at our reflection for hours.
And as this dream comes to an end, dear fairies,
we'll sail down a gentle stream,
I'll awake to find my rested soul,
oh, how I would love such a dream!

March 6, 2004
Track from Via Poetica *CD*

Bandage

I need to place a bandage on my heart,
and special thread to mend what feels so broken.
I need to be sure you understand my feelings,
of words and ways that may have gone unspoken.
I need to take a tangible remnant of you,
and sew it in a quilt of special faces,
so when your absence becomes my reality,
I can wrap myself within those joyous places,
that you and I had shared for just a little while,
but never long enough could that ever be,
for you, dear friend, my love will be forever,
and all our memories will last an eternity.

May 20, 2004

Heaven's Colors

I would dance with you if I could,
fly high above the clouds and touch rainbows with my fingertips,
never hoping for a pot of gold,
but more of a glimpse of what Heaven's colors must truly be.
That's where you are. You come to me
as a spectrum of light through a window,
and as a scent of your remembered fragrance in the wind.
Ever such a slight glimmer of hope of what Heaven must be.
And on earth it is for me
these simple wishes and sights I feel in my soul's eyes
I will hold with me until my hand touches yours,
and we dance high above the clouds,
never to be apart again.

September 10, 2004
Track from Via Poetica *CD*

Upon seeing
The Passion of the Christ

I have been awakened.

Now You cross my mind in a way unimaginable.

This love is humbling and pure,

and I know that no path is too hard to cross,

with You beside me,

for You have already bared every cross

I could ever stumble upon.

As I fail myself, as I fall,

it is Your hand I feel in mine,

lifting me up,

offering me forgiveness.

It is with this unconditional love I can stand,

with my magnificent soul and know

with all my heart,

I am never alone,

and always loved by You.

September 13, 2004

"Heart, mind, and now I'm 'souled'
on the blessings of God's
Infinite wisdom.
No longer am I a caged creation.
I have paid high prices,
replaced guilt with gratefulness,
flung open the windows
and have simply flown away"

September 2004

"I am but an hourglass,
and each second I live, breathe, give,
and be me,
is but a grain of sand.
As it descends down,
the wings of my soul float
higher and higher!...
As we grow older,
it is our ego that must fall away,
for our wisdom
to take flight!"

August 2004
Track from Via Poetica *CD*

You, to Me

You, to me, are a blessing bestowed upon the earth,
Planted deep into my soul,
And I will love you, and love you, and love you.
You are the faith that keeps my head held high,
Spreading a beacon of hope
That surrounds me with warmth and light,
And I will love you, and love you, and love you,
Always.

April 2004

Soon

Soon I will hold a miracle.
She will squeeze my one finger, in her delicate hand,
with a grasp that amazes me, and, at the same time,
let's me know how she feels inside.
And without one single word spoken from her tiny lips,
that touch will tell me how much
she needs me and loves me.
Me. Mom. Soon.

October 2004

Intoxicated

I have to remind myself to move,
to speak, and to breathe when I'm around you.
It is as if I were standing in a forest of woodland creatures,
and if I move too suddenly,
I will frighten you away.
How can my heart tell my mouth what to say
when I fear if I do let the words slip off my tongue,
you'll see my vulnerability.
Now that I have breathed you in and have become so
intoxicated by your beauty,
how do I dare let this sweet sensation leave my lungs?
I capture your soft image in my mind to gaze upon
when you are not near me,
and every word you have ever spoken,
has been permanently recorded in my heart.

May 20, 2005
Track from Via Poetica *CD*

Go Deep Within

Go deep within and meander through your heart,
opening doors you once closed,
or, once in a while, gave a peek through.
And there you'll find your soul,
shining as brilliant as diamonds!
Walk through that door. Be brave!
Take time to discover you!...
To bless, love and be you.

April 16, 2005
Track From Via Poetica *CD*

This is What Peace Tastes Like

This is what peace tastes like –
it melts on your tongue,
sends fragrant breezes through your hair,
and lingers like a beautiful love song,
in the whispering corridors of your mind.

April 16, 2005

This is What I Have to Offer You

It is not just physical, it is spiritual.
It is not about outer appearance, but inner appearance.
When I wrap my arms around you,
I wrap myself in a love so great
only God Himself could have created.
You are beauty.
You are light,
and I am yours for eternity.
I will seek you out, and you will do the same,
just for one touch of you,
anywhere, anytime.
It is true. It is me, and it is you,
because, my love, we are one.
And this is what I have to offer you.

April 29, 2005

"I have been awakened by Love, and I shall never sleep again.
I need not slumber for you infuse me with peace.
Your essence is tranquility and joy!
Let me never go back to the land of the sleeping.
Here with you I remember I can fly!"

April 2006

"We cannot afford to waste time on words.
We must spend time sharing our emotions
that originate from our hearts,
and resonate in our souls."

2004

"Our souls are the children of the world,
and our words are their playthings.
Let's play nicely with one another and
use our words with kindness."

June 2005

Where Should My Arms Reach Out

Where should my arms reach out to embrace you?
I hold them as wide open as I can and imagine
a spiritual being standing there.
This person in my dreams never speaks,
yet fills me with light and love.
We dance, as in olden days, a Waltz,
two gazes meshed into one.
This is a world I cannot seem to find on Earth,
but it does exist.
I know how to get there with my eyes closed.
I know this is love. I know this is what I want.
If only I could sleep forever, I would be where I need to be,
with someone I do not know, do not need to know,
yet I do know –
a soul which lies in you, whoever you are,
I await your return. I await your physical form,
so my arms can reach out and embrace you,
my true love.

May 19, 2005
Track from Via Poetica *CD*
https://www.youtube.com/watch?v=EqOohrtmmqk
Dedicated to Sean Fuller, my beloved husband
We finally found each other

What Could Be More Beautiful than Love?

What could be more beautiful than Love?
A perfection of nature,
the perfect rainstorm,
the answer to an angel's prayer.
You.
Just perfection –
inside and out, outside and in,
but, oh to taste within is to taste
life's sweetest nectar
any bee could create,
nor rosebud could bloom,
no singer could sing with complete accuracy.
You are perfection.
What could be more beautiful than Love?
What could be more beautiful than you?

June 18, 2005

Awakened Souls

I have united with my spirit,
my beautiful soul,
and I am one with oneness.
Yet not alone,
as many masses awaken one another.
And with awakened souls,
one by one,
we feel and experience oneness,
discovering and sharing truth, love, and peace,
spreading as vast as the beams of the sun,
pure masses of radiant light,
freeing the Earth from pain,
swallowing fear with courage,
and moving forward as powerful as thunder,
once and for all...
with love, with life, and with God.

June 14, 2005

"My heart and soul will
not let this end,
for it breathes life
Into me."

August 2005

❧

"To see your face
is to see many faces of all you've ever been.
To see your soul
is to see only one soul of all you ever were
and all you'll always be –
truly magnificent!"

September 2005

❧

"Let me give you
one day of my life filled with
lifetimes of my love.
Each moment building a cathedral of peace
for you to reside in
when the day is done."

October 2005

I Want You and Only You in my Life

Just to know that you know
how great it makes me feel when you run your fingers
through my hair,
or the way I frown when I stupidly hang a picture crooked,
you know just what to say.
And no matter how annoyed I become at you,
even though you are not at fault,
you try to seek a deep meaning,
seeing the frustration within me, and understanding me,
sometimes when I fail to understand myself.
And through your unconditional love,
you forgive me and love me.
I want that in my life, whether I vow with a ring on my finger,
or not.
I want you and only you, and this is just to let you know,
that for these reasons and many more,
why I love you.

October 2, 2004
Dedicated to Sean, my beloved

Let Me Forever Live

Let me forever live in the happiness of this moment,
as I stand as one and as still among the trees,
filled with a united peace and serenity.
Here in this moment, I see God.
I hear God.
I am one of God with God.
May I forever live and be
a soul flying free,
with the currents of the wind as my sails,
ascending higher and higher,
to hear the beautiful songs of the angels,
caressing my being and remembering me
with eternal life.

December 28, 2005

"May God's wings lift you up
to smell the aromas from Heaven's kitchen,
to taste the splendor of life.
May it replenish your soul's appetite
to live on Mother Earth,
and walk with contentment
in your heart."

❧

"Sometimes we become like dry sponges
that just need to absorb a few
raindrops from Heaven
to be brought back to our 'Selves'
when we are being our self."

❧

"When happiness becomes our necessity,
the TV will be shut off, eyes will meet,
and souls will share.
Let us focus our attention on the comedy
playing all around us.
It's a five-star movie!"

September 2005

My Love Forever Runs to You

My love forever runs to you.
It finds you.
It seeks you out with a vision that can only be seen
from the stars.
The sound of your voice travels to Heaven's ears,
and presents itself back to me in the most
Divine gift to my soul,
filling me with your love, your laughter,
your face, your smile,
and, once again, you bless me with your presence.
I'll forever find you.
I'll forever seek you out,
because, my love,
we truly are one.

December 10, 2005
Dedicated to Sean, my beloved

"I saw you,
and you were beautiful.
I spoke to you,
and you were kind.
I loved you,
but you never heard me speak it.
And I'm sorry
you never heard it said."

January 2006
Dedicated to Marjorie Swift

Full Moon Fairy

A moon fairy by starlight shall fly tonight,
encircling all from whence she sees,
in a double helix through spirit trees,
and fairy dust shall bless you! And fairy dust shall bless you!
A moon fairy's eyes speak with such grace,
singing, if you listen, ever near,
"Let your fingertips embrace, what seems to be an empty space,"
there among sleeping flowers,
for seemingly countless hours,
and fairy dust shall bless you! And fairy dust shall bless you!
Oh behold, my dear one, what lies within,
before your waking hours,
how all has been released for you,
between your waking hours.
Thou hast manifest a miracle,
and power shall rise within,
and fairy dust has blessed you! And fairy dust has blessed you!

January 14, 2005
Track from Via Poetica *CD*

The Fairy and the Gnome

The exquisite fairy stood on the top of a stalk of Rosemary in the summer sun and exclaimed to the gnome, "I challenge you to find something stronger than love!"

With a smirk on his face of determination, he began his quest journeying over the planet to find a source stronger than love. But as he traveled miles upon miles, he felt defeated. Saddened, he bent his head low to pray and out of the blue he heard a voice say, "Fly back and hold her in your arms", and he did just that. He walked right up to her being with a fierce feeling of confidence in his eyes, reached his arms out to her and embraced the beautiful fairy to his own being and said, "I have searched far and wide and have found that the love I feel right here in my heart is the strongest love that I will ever find."

She smiled sweetly and knowingly as she embraced him back and said, "What took you so long?"

April 2, 2012

"Breathe in the softness
of each moment,
like the sunset
slipping under the sheets
of the deep, blue sea –
warm, safe and loved."

October 2005

❧

"To understand the many doors of life,
we must first walk through and experience
what's behind them.
Don't just peek.
Swing them wide open with joy in your heart!
Take it all in.
Be grateful and
keep walking tall
until the next door appears."

January 2006

My Gift to You

My gift to you is sacred.
It comes to you through the arms of Mother Earth,
and penetrates your senses,
and within those moments,
you hear me and see me,
and healing pours into your being.
Your gift to me is sacred.
It is kept safe inside my soul.
It comes to me like ocean waves,
replenishing me in return,
and healing pours into my being.

January 21, 2006
Dedicated to Sean, my beloved

It is

I have a wish for the world.
It is...
to kiss the hands of Mother Earth by reaching for –
the boughs of branches, the rocks of streams,
the touch of petals, and the grace when starlight captivates
your sight.
It is...
the scent of a rose that brings you back to someone's arms
you miss so much, more than words can say.
It is...
teardrops falling down your cheeks when you witness the miracle
of birth, and the sadness of rebirth.
It is, and always has been my wish for us to truly know life just as
it is...
a crashing wave that fills you up with the power of the Universe,
and sends you dreaming of all we can be tomorrow,
and all we really are today.
It is... my wish. It is... all we need to know.

January 29, 2006
Track from Via Poetica *CD*

New Moon Fairy

Princess, oh princess, what shall you bring?
The heart of the angels, the sweetest of Spring?
"I shall bring darkness so light can then flow,
to all the lost beings walking below."
Princess, oh princess, what will you do?
"Teach them that kindness is but a stem from me to you.
As you sleep under covers and grow with each day,
the heart of the moon is guiding your way.
Your inner child, forever strengthened,
and wishes are blessed, those dreams and dear longings,
earth angels manifest."
Princess, oh princess, shall we see you again?
"As each new moon arises, I shall bless you, my friend."

January 29, 2006
Dedicated to Kia Rondeau

A little girl walked up to me at a Carnival and out of the blue, while licking her vanilla ice cream cone, she said to me, "I like things that are like sugar." Lick. Smile. Lick. She was so adorable! I looked down and said, "Well, that is really a nice thing to love!" And she said, "Yuppers! I just do!" As for me, I was waiting in line to throw a paid dart at a target I was sure I would miss. And then she asked, "Would you like some of my ice cream?" and for a long, long second many thoughts sped through my head, like the thought of germs and bacteria and who is this child!? But in those brief seconds I surprised myself and said "Yes!"! And with a tiny lick, I tasted that sweet vanilla ice cream on my tongue and a huge Cheshire cat smile spread across my face. It tasted so sweet and wonderful! She looked up at me with a smile that matched mine ten thousand-fold! We stood looking into each other's eyes for a long moment and then I threw my dart. Without thinking, I just let it fly and it hit solid to the target! The man looked at me and said, "Congrats! Pick a prize from this wall!" Oh! I was so shocked! "Wow!" I said. And then I looked down at her, this sweet little light of love and said, "You pick whatever you would like." She leaned over the booth with an enormous grin, gave a good hard look and finally said, "That one!" And bouncing up and down in her tiny flats she soon held a black and white striped Zebra, much bigger than her own self! I laughed a hearty, joyful laugh and finally said, "And why that one?!" With little kisses on her Zebra's cheeks, she said in a light whisper, "They are black and white together." As she walked away with her cone and new friend, I thought to myself such wisdom through the eyes of a child.

August 27, 2018

Belonging

I don't know where I am.
I am following an imaginary stream of light,
hoping it will lead me to peace.
I don't know where I belong.
Perhaps it is not here.
I wander in my mind, picking daisies and wistfully blue,
I look for brighter tomorrows,
and I see me, and I see you,
seeing me in depth, in color, in grace.
I wonder if connection to spirit,
has been lost due to static in space.
And who is this person in the mirror that
fills that empty space,
so filled with cotton balls and wine,
dry and unsatisfied with a quench that no river could fill.
I once was a puzzle with beautifully shaped pieces,
full of hope and promise.
I stare down at the empty caverns and
wonder what happened,
to the riches that once lay within me.
Who has those pieces?
How do I put them back where they belong?

(continued...)

Who will want to hold me, these badly damaged pieces
that they are?
Who will wipe away the layers of pain, sorrow,
unforgiveness and loneliness,
that has plastered a very dismal mask on my face.
Will anyone ever be able to see beyond the ugliness,
despair, and heartache?
I wonder where I am right now in the Universe.
At least I believe that beyond the veil is peace, light, love, and grace.
Maybe that is where I belong.
Bring me to light.
Bring me to love.
Bring me to happiness.
Bring me to You,
Here is my hand. I beg of You, take it!
Bring me to home.

February 2006
Track from Via Poetica *CD*

God's Ears

Stars are the ears of the Universe.
What is it that we wish to tell them?
Shooting stars are for the whispered words we speak.
It will take time to understand,
what we cannot comprehend.
It will take time for our wishes to come true.
It is the stars transparent appearance during the day,
that fools our human eyes,
but the stars are listening,
always listening.
So, let's use words that are
as magnificent as stars.
Let them sparkle and light up the Heavens,
and with patience,
we can evolve to understand
their power and ours,
coexisting in universal harmony and peace.

February 17, 2006

You are the Wind

You are the wind,
and I am the tree that dances in your breath.
Without you, I am still,
and motionless,
patiently waiting to be moved.
Your breeze lets me sway,
and be playful, and happy.
Rooted by your presence,
and caressed in your warm breezes,
you carry my fragrant blossoms,
through the air and fill the world with love.
You empower me with the strength to bend,
and still stand tall.
I am blessed to be able to share my love with you,
in such a graceful way,
and I thank you with gentle bows in return.

May 10, 2006
Track from Via Poetica *CD*

Atlantis Rising (Vesperia Epilogue)

The sun is rising.
I feel it touching my face.
It is Source. It is God. It is you. It is me.
Warmth penetrating my being.
My steps reach out with toes aligned to Earth,
knowing it is where I must go, and there,
I am,
breathing, breathing, breathing.
Inhale –
Exhale.
I am ready to receive, and yet ready to let go.
You are ALL,
this I feel and know.
I walk your paths so carefully cleared.
I see what I need, want, and desire.
It all stems back to You –
circles, spirals, roundness of woman,
of life,
it never ends.

(continued...)

It continues.
It draws, colors, creates,
and re-creates what it wishes,
without question or wonder.
As I send out, I await your response.
It comes gently to my ears,
as a caressing wind, a leaf cascading to the ground,
and I am filled with here and now,
love and joy,
tomorrow and today.
And in this moment,
I am blessed,
as I breathe in what I long for,
I receive.
I embrace You, and I thank You.

March 3, 2006
Closing track of Richard Bone's Vesperia *CD, May 3, 2006*
https://www.youtube.com/watch?v=3BKVU6ocPdQ
https://www.youtube.com/watch?v=1UQ4FX-NU68

How I Wish to Fly!

I have often wished that I could fly,
and have searched for my wings far and wide,
as I've watched the angels dance above me
with elegance and grace,
and embraced me in a featherbed of love,
casting their light upon all I've been dreaming of.
How I wish to fly!
To know life with a view that only the stars can offer.
They wink and blink like happy secret keepers,
with their joyous smiles,
always looking filled with contentment and peace.
I wish upon them for such sweet release.
Tonight, I shall dream that I am one of them.
I shall sparkle and shine with a knowingness,
that all I need to do to be in this moment is
breathe! Breathe in the breath of life,
all the while knowing it is but a dream,
but a dream of what I can and will become,
a shining star with wings, under the sun, and off I shall go!

May 2006
Two Tracks from Via Poetica *CD (Goddess Mix – final track)*

"Sometimes the light that
pours into us
is not by the rays of the sun,
but by the source of Love's essence
flowing into one another."

June 2006

❧

"Let me feed your soul,
for it craves an attention
all its own,
and I understand its
needs, wants, and desires."

March 2007

❧

"Your presence delicately enhances my being."

May 2007

❧

"See with the eyes of your heart.
Feel with the gentleness of a butterfly.
Sip the sweet nectar life gratefully."

May 2007

Visibly Invisible Love

It isn't the kind of thing you'd often read in a newspaper.
Love rarely is.
It follows you home when you think you are alone.
You speak to it in darkness,
and at red lights,
and wish it was, physically,
your best friend,
that presence you cannot see,
yet you know is quite there,
sweetly lingering,
holding onto the steering wheel,
while you wonder where tomorrow went,
and where you are off to today,
such a divine presence that keeps you,
here and now,
on your path to Light.

August 2007

"Beloved,
you need to take time,
sometimes,
to gaze more deeply
into my eyes,
for at times my love is
shy and afraid.
You need to take time,
sometimes,
to feel what is not tangible,
yet as soft as my skin.
Oh love,
I am here,
more here than you visibly see.
See me now and always."

"I never knew beauty was a feeling until I met you."

October 2007
Dedicated to Sean, my beloved

The Longing for a Lover's Kiss

The longing for a lover's kiss forever lingers,
if the wish was never fulfilled,
until the soul is released from its vacant shell,
and returns, once again,
to the universal sea of infinite hopes and possibilities.
Like the soul, the longing for this kiss never dies,
yet patiently waits for the kiss that was never felt,
the sacred touch that never graced,
the hungry beloved's skin.
Ah, but in this here, imagination lives on and on,
and for an illusion of time,
the connection of tender, caressing skin to skin is made,
and a love can be felt in that moment of being,
and the presence for the longing of a lover's kiss,
forever lingering in a mind, body, and soul,
in temporary satisfaction for the longing,
is fulfilled.

Jun 30, 2009

"All the bravest dive into the ocean waves
knowing they will eventually reach the shore.
Once that example is set,
others follow,
even if they just get their feet wet."

January 2012

"It is within the sanctuary of the beckoning light
that we find refuge
on the peaceful shores."

"You can seek knowledge in volumes of books
for infinite wisdom,
but the best inspiration seldom discovered
is written between the pages
of the human heart.
Open this book and be nourished."

How Do You Keep an Earth Angel

How do you keep an earth angel,
when she has wings to fly?
You don't.
You may bask in her light for many moments of time,
and feel the warmth of her heavenly sunshine,
for she is like an elusive butterfly.
And when you cry,
she opens those wings,
and an angelic voice sings its heavenly song.
Never seek to hold those angel's wings too tightly,
for when she is able to fly,
wherever she goes,
far and wide,
love and peace will fill many hearts,
and heal many souls.

October 6, 2012
Dedicated to all the beautiful earth angels of peace

"Seeing is feeling.
Speaking puts seeing into the heart of believing
that what does not seem real is more real
than we can possibly imagine!"

※

"Capture what you can,
and what you cannot will be captured for you in another lifetime.
Just believe that your net is magic and eventually it will happen.
The Universe has no wrong replies."

March 2012

※

"He walked with a half step combined with a whole.
It was musical to me.
I found this song springing from my lips, chant-like in nature...
'peace will.. make the...world go... 'round'.'"

April 2012

※

"Love is not the answer because it was never a question.
It just simply is – a pure, living, breathing energy
that will exist forever."

August 2012

An Alzheimer's Request

If we look into the mirror,
and you see me staring there,
don't wonder where I am,
instead, just touch and brush my hair.
And if you see me, absently, gazing into space,
just know that all my angels,
comfort me in this new place.
My love for you it will not die,
And cannot for, you see
for I am part of you,
and you, forever, a part of me.

April 2013
Dedicated to Jeannette Bouchard, "Aunt Jean"
I miss you

"I have a hunger for what is not planted on the face of the earth.
This seed lies deep within our souls.
There is no field nor pasture where it will sprout,
for this seed lives eternally inside us.
It wishes to be heard.
I dare say it is lonely for
its proper attention and balance
within the Universe."

October 2013

"Perception is a prism
that differs at all stages of life.
But if love is at the center of the stage,
the show will go on to
a standing ovation!"

October 2013

I Love You

I love you.
It is not like the love
for candy or ice cream,
nor swings or a slide.
It is the kind of love that has no wish
to run and hide,
just bask in sunlight,
when no rays seem near,
it is warm and penetrating,
Oh, I love you so dear.

October 11, 2013

The Tree of Life

And in a moment so silent,

Love grew,

like a tree yearning to feel the sun.

It grew so tall that it could not stop itself as it rose into the Universe.

Love reached up so high that it began to wonder, "does it ever end?"

And the Universe took Love's hand and said,

"This is just the beginning.

Walk with me and let me hold you close.

We have so much to explore in a never-ending journey called
the Tree of Life."

November 1, 2013

The Daisy

On such a lovely sunny day, a daisy created such a display.
She arched her back, popping out each petal of white,
to the rising sun's warmth and delight.
So proud she did bloom and once she was done,
she basked in the warmth of the springtime sun.
And as she contently spread out her wings,
she began hearing a voice of sad feelings,
a young woman, so lovely, but sad of times,
began talking to the daisy with tears in her eyes.
"I wish I were like you, so blissful and full.
I feel so lifeless, so ugly, so dull."
The daisy arched her way and let out a sigh,
and said, "Oh my dear, why do you cry?
You are God's creation, and so that is why,
You are perfectly imperfect, as so am I!"
And the daisy took a petal that was longer than them all,
and parted the others so it would stand tall.
"You see this one petal? It is longer than the rest,
and as far as I can see, this is my best."
The young woman was touched, to her heart this did speak,
and in a small pond she gazed down and gave a long peek.
"Yes, I believe you are right! How silly of me,
to think I was less than God had made me!"
The daisy bowed her stem, tucked the petal back in its place,
as the young woman shared a smile on her happy face.
And there they both stayed, so peaceful and light,
as the full moon slowly rose, their spirits took flight!

2018

A woman quietly walked along the shores of a lake, waded into the water up to her knees and began to share her thoughts aloud.

"I hate getting old! I'm losing all my color! Why do we fade so? My lips are not so red, my hair more and more white. It saddens me so."

At that very moment, an enormous emerald, green frog appeared. He had been listening to every word.

"My dear lady, none of those colors have ever left you, for inside your heart is where they are and have always resided. And over the years you have chosen to share some of your color with every kiss you gave, and your hair for every lover's stroke of its soft, fine texture, a bit of color was blessed to each beloved you gave your heart to so unselfishly. But, my dear lady, please know that in return they filled your heart with their colors of love so it can never be depleted."

"Really?!"

"Really," the frog replied.

A soft smile came across her face.

"You are a wise frog."

"And YOU are, and always will be, a beautiful woman!"

And love has a heart of its own. It beats like the largest star throughout the universe and pulsates into each of us. Like telepathic highways to the soul.

"Ring!" ....

"Hello?" ...

"I just called to say I love you!"

Ahhh, the sweetest slices of starshine served on a plate of wine-drenched sauce filling each belly with what is a most sincere, nurturing meal. Savor each bite, nibble, sip.

December 12, 2013

"You are the oars of a lifeboat that
stroke the delicate waves of my skin,
skimming the surface,
and leaving magnificent ripples cascading
to the very bottom of my soul,
forever suspended in a loving embrace
of peace."

August 2014

The Winter Butterfly

Lest not my soul waste a moment,
for I have lived beyond my thoughts and dreams.
Lest not my heart skip a beat,
for it spreads my wings to fly through the snowflakes of Winter.
How am I still here? Alive!
Is it a midsummer dream?
Or am I really in spirit, living in a fairy tale
of soon to be read pages of life.
Ah, how very brisk, the air, yet it is not from
nature's intention to harm,
nor does it hinder me in my being.
I cannot return to what was, that warm cocoon.
I must venture on!
I shall follow with the compass of my dreams,
pointed in the direction of love and live on!
Love and live as if it is but a dream.

December 16, 2013

A Recipe to Help Someone Ill

Hold the intent to heal.
Feel them in your arms.
Wrap them in your light.
Tell them how much you care.
Make them chicken soup or,
a giant bowl of their favorite ice cream.
Listen to all they have to say, even if they are asleep.
Massage them with Arnica Oil.
Fluff their pillows during needed naps,
but above all, whisper in their beautiful ears,
"I love you."

December 6, 2013

"There is a gentleness in winter, as there is in spring,
all flow entwined into all our being.
We see, we hear, we sense in life,
The beauty around us,
through our glories and strife,
but, above all, we can say, we have lived!
Ah! To live!
To spread your wings in the summer sun,
until fall casts down the first leaf.
Yes, I am. Beloved I am."

December 21, 2013

"*I love you* like a timeless wind that knows just where to blow
to find your being.
I want you with the force of a dolphin leaping from the ocean waves.
I adore you like the first toy given to a little girl From Santa Claus.
That's how much I love you."

February 14, 2014

"*I love you* like...
Wonder Woman loves her cape,
And Popeye loves spinach, for strength when he aches.
Spaghetti loves meatballs, and lasagna loves cheese,
The Sandman loves sleepy eyes, and the flowers love bees."

February 12, 2014

"*I love you...* like delicious chocolate chip cookies on steroids,
And stars with millions of Energizer Bunny batteries,
making them the size of enormous, glowing pearls in the sky!
So, let's grab a tall, cool glass of milk,
and dip, dunk, and dance in the moonlight!
Oops! You gotta little chocolate on your cheek!
'Lick!' ... all gone!"

February 13, 2014

The Dragon and the Little Girl

For surely you are not a beast, but a sea horse that breathes fire!
Come smell this flower's essence and swing with me
higher and higher!"
she gleefully said to the dragon of the sky,
and with a smile on his face of scales he did reply –
"Oh, surely, I shall take a whiff, but must watch you as you sway,
take a jump as you swing forward and let us be on our way!"
"To where and whence, dear dragon? This island is all I know.
I am but meek and small, will this journey help me grow?"
He winked with lashes that seemed miles in length,
and gave a toothy grin,
and for a tiny second or so she sensed a sulfur wind.
"This is but a steppingstone, a rock along your path,
journeys have many layers, come sit upon my back."
And something stirred inside her heart, not letting her mind decide,
she nimbly crawled upon the dragon's back and gaze a delicate sigh.
And off they went to live out dreams, and soak in the sun of life,
oh, such a marriage is born each day beyond a man and wife.
(To be continued...)

February 19, 2014

The Dragon and the Little Girl

He was weary, steps heavy and his soul feeling so depleted. His tail swayed sadly behind his scaled body. Why such heaviness? Oh yes, she stopped believing in him at some point.

Or so he thought.

He wandered over to her little swing and gave it a nudge with his pinky finger which, of course, sent it flying like a yo-yo around the thick tree branch. Where did she go? He knew she had grown since his last journey with her, but he felt so lost without her. Oh! The feel of her flying on his scaled back, singing so carefree in the summer winds as they traveled all over their imaginary world.

And just as he was about to fly away, she appeared! She was all grown up and quite lovely. She squinted for a moment, as one would when bright sunlight dazzles one's sight, and then she gave a huge Cheshire cat smile and exclaimed, "Oh! You came back! Oh, how I've missed you!"

He was confused, for he had never completely left, but in her amazing growth, so overnight, she had lost sight, just a bit, but now it all came flying back to her – the peaceful solace of pure enchantment!

"Can I still go on a journey with you?" she asked.

And with his sulfur-scented smile, he grinned and said,

"Your chariot awaits, me lady."

And off they went!

February, 2014

Like the clay in his hands, he molded me with his love; formed a cup to drink from to quench his longing, and a spoon to feed his hungry mouth. He created the beauty he saw within my eyes with his gentle love. How do I deny what I see before me in a mirror, the truth of who I am and how he makes me feel... beautiful!

February 4, 2015

Love ... reads, writes, and speaks in tones of colorful chords. You are an instrument of God! You create love songs every day with a simple smile, a hello from the wave of your hand, a warm hug from your arms, and a tender kiss on someone's lips. What will you sing today to me? Oh, what shall you sing?

May 25, 2014

❀

"Oh yes!" the angel said, "when the journey is new, the first step through that door is like being reborn! We understand... it's a new venture, a new chapter. But how dull of a life you would live if you kept reading the same chapter of your ever-evolving book of life? Still, we encourage you, walk through that door! What do you have to lose? Love is all that truly exists. Leave the pain behind, dear one. A new adventure awaits to begin!

November 29, 2013

Not the News

As for me, I shall watch Autumn leaves sway -
not the news.
Laughing children in fallen leaves, at play –
not the news.
I shall see the starlight twinkle stark bright –
not the news.
The geese flying bravely in flight –
not the news.
I shall feel the Autumn breeze on my face –
not the news.
Hot soups and breads that fill me with amazing grace –
not the news.

October 1, 2014

"Love is gracious in its true form.
It wears no costume; it is unmasked.
It walks in no shoes, just the skin of the soul.
And in its sacred grace we are divinely blessed."

June 2014

"Seasons... one sheds the coat of winter
to make love to the heart of summer.
The other to add a coat of summer
to make love to the heart of winter."

August 2015

"You are a gift to the Universe
that can never be duplicated,
yet shared by a million stars of light with love."

August 2015

The Treasure Chest

I found a box, strong and sturdy,
it didn't matter that it wasn't pretty.
I opened up its cardboard lid,
and blew some love and peace within.
Kisses and squishes, warm smiles to share,
within this box I laid them there.
And on your grave there sat this chest
of love and wishes I did my best,
to give you back what you gave to me,
a love so true for eternity.

October 1, 2014

And there she sat; her feet neatly tucked beneath her denim ripped blue jeans. She was engrossed in her task. I walked gingerly into the room, like a ballerina entering stage right, and watched her as she carefully gathered each little shred of paper and, one by one, began the painstaking task of gluing them all back together. Before her, a mound of white with scribbled ink. After a moment, I decided to sit beside her and help. She was despondent to my actions but did not stop me all the same. We glued, piece by piece, for hours until my back ached. Finally, the last shred of paper was in place. She sighed and looked up at me.

"It's not easy, you know."
"What isn't, dear one?" I asked.
"This gluing, all the time!"
I looked at her, confused. And then, as she sadly walked away, she said, "Turn the paper over... you'll see."

And as I watched her walk away, I saw the soft, angelic outline of two wings between her shoulder blades. With a tear in my eye, I gazed down at the large sheet and saw that it was like a paint-by-number of figures and data, all written like codes of DNA strands. I gently placed my hand at the corner of this sheet and carefully flipped it over. There, to my astonishment, staring back at me were thousands of faces, souls who lost their lives fighting for our country. In the center was a picture of her father. And written in tiny letters underneath were the words

"Pieces of My Heart".

"One star is an integral part of a constellation,
and whether it feels like the end, or the beginning does not matter.
What matters only to the sky is that it chooses to SHINE and
become One with the Universe."

September 2015

❊

"I stood on the brink and knew that nothing would be the same again.
All I had to do was throw away my crutches into the sky –
those imaginary addictions, phobias, and sad thoughts
holding me back with fear.
I let them go, looked down at my legs and
felt them move freely on their own!
I learned, with God's love, that I could fly!"

September 2014

❊

"If I had only one kiss I could give to you, I would send it to all the
stars in Heaven, so that every night you would forever be tenderly
touched by my lips with a kiss goodnight."

July 2014

"Beauty is an element that walks beside the soul so no one can miss the aura of its Divine light."

October 2017

❈

"It's not that you are letting go. You're just letting the kite sail higher into the sky. If you never let a kite be what a kite is meant to be, it sadly remains in your hands on a white string. But if you let it be what it is meant to be, you give it the freedom to fly, and still that white string stays attached keeping you grounded, yet free to be who truly are!"

July 2014

❈

"New dreams are not born from living in yesterday's shadows. They are born from seeing tomorrow with the eyes of the rising sun."

October 2016

"What is Love?
Love is the cosmos swirling in your heart.
It is the ever-changing domino through space,
taking your breath away with its divine power."

2013

"Don't dance too long in the shadows of your life,
for while they may make you seem larger than life,
the true you that is dancing is how we wish to see you.
The shadow you see beside you simply dances because you do."

September 2015

Good Morning, My Love!

It may have been a weekday,
but that simply mattered little,
as I awoke to see her beautiful face
and felt a joyful giggle.
The automatic brewer
was busy as a bee,
brewing aromatic java
for my love and me.
Yes, time stands still each morning,
as I gaze and see her there.
No matter what each sunrise brings
I wish to be right here."

August 2015
Dedicated to Tom and "Pinky" Gregson

She Weeps Such Pretty Tears

She weeps such pretty tears.
They make me want to stay.
But in my heart, I know,
I've already gone away.
I think I remember her name,
somewhere not long ago,
It seems like such a shame,
And as I think about tomorrow,
and she weeps a little more,
I will not remember me,
my mind is closing the door.
Oh, my pretty weeper,
this hasn't been my choice,
for whomever has become my governor
has taken away my voice.
But before I completely slip away,
you'll see me weeping too.
With all the love within my heart,
I'll always be loving you."

January 2016
Dedicated to Aunt Carol and to all the victims
of Alzheimer's and dementia

"I dare say, if a whisper of peace
had the power of the wind,
true freedom
would live throughout the world."

January 2016

"You don't need a fancy shoe to leave a loving footprint on someone's heart. You just need to place your feet firmly on that sacred ground and tell your heart that you were loved by this soul, for a few precious moments of time. No wind or rain shall sweep away that pathway of love if it was real. You simply set a path of light to guide others to follow."

February 2016

"Even in the face of what seems like dark days is just a perception, for the sun does not take time off. If you stop to feel the warmth of the sun, you can feel it. The light of it forever lives in our hearts and throughout the world."

February 2017

"Lazy hours of the soul.
Tattletales whispered from ancient blooms.
One's heart needs rest to restore the inner light.
New laughter shall burst with fond delight!"

June 2020

False Flattery

I had a dear friend, he treated me well,
poetry of old, and stories to tell.
With enticing dialogue, I believed it all,
like candy to a child, I took the fall.
How cunning, how savvy, his speeches he did make,
as the fly slowly creeps up, a sly web he did make.
And in a swoop so convincing, with truths twisted like silk,
I was within a masked face, in this false web that he built.
But nay I am far wiser, though sticky as t'was,
I forfeited my hand and let go of what was.
That now dull, false illusion he once showered upon me,
has taught me the lesson of false flattery.

2016

As I was prepping dinner, a huge fly kept "flirting" with me, rather annoyingly (let's just say, good thing I'm not a hungry spider). And then, as I watched it, I decided I should 'shift my perception', even just for a moment, and see this fly through the eyes of love.

Well, that's all it took. You know that saying, "I wish I was a fly on the wall?" Sounds kinda strange, but here is what this fly had to say:

"You humans waste so much food. We flies understand this and adore your garbage for that reason. It is an astronomical feast of great proportions, not to mention your compost heaps, landfills, and scraps you throw into the ocean. And that's just the tip of the iceberg!

And although you loath us, we fly around swiftly, watch, and listen to what you do. We are not afraid to enter your dwellings, unlike dragon flies – they observe from a distance."

I replied, "But why do you come into our homes?"

"Ah! We serve as constant reminders to 'waste not; want not'. And you humans still have not learned. Also, the invaluable lesson of what it truly means to share all that you have with every being that exists. Our life span is much shorter, yet we understand this invaluable quality."

I sighed. "You make a valid point."

He sat on my windowsill, looked at me for a moment and then flew out the sliding glass doors. Nature has so much to teach us!

May 20, 2016

A Gift to a Stranger

I gave a stranger a Christmas gift, never wrapped beneath my tree,
as much as I love to give to all if was a present from Jesus, not me.
For some moments in life are chosen for us to bless others
in mysterious ways,
to teach us about God's forgiveness and bring awareness to our days,
of what is truly precious and what cannot be replaced,
to reach beyond the physical and remember amazing grace.
So, I gave my purse to a stranger, and heard his voice inside me say,
"I'm sorry, please forgive me, but I saw no other way."
And a serenity began to fill my heart and to this voice I did reply –
"Reach inside my wallet and you'll find a small card inside
with a picture and a prayer and perhaps on Christmas day,
you'll give a gift back to Jesus and find another way".
My purse has been replaced and I am safe and well,
and where this stranger is right now only God can ever tell.
But I truly forgive you, stranger, I bless and send you light,
so you may see it shining over you for guidance day and night.

2017

I Dreamed I Was an Angel

I dreamed I was an angel with wings that spanned the sky.
I listened to concerns of Presidents,
and whispered prayers of Popes gone by,
the silent yearn of children, the longing for a lover's touch,
and tranquil, tender words in life that soothe and heal so much;
to guide the bees, the bears, the wolves,
and the sweetest songs of birds,
the rolling roar of thunder and trembling ground of herds.
I dreamed I was an angel but soon realized as I did,
as an earth angel I had one mission,
a mission to forgive,
and to offer human compassion –
a song, a poem, a praise,
a hug, a kiss, an ear
to listen for better ways
of all we can, in time, become as hand in hand we join,
through a portal of opportunity,
our magical golden coin.

April 17, 2018

Let There Be No More Painful Prayer

Let there be no more painful prayer
for God has heard your cries,
the Lord is walking beside you,
wiping tears from beneath your eyes.
For it is only when we see our lives
through the lens of a cloudy view
that frightens us with illusions of
what simply is not true.
For God loves every one of us as we travel on,
in a never-ending story that we have free will to build upon.
God is always at the helm, though at times we feel betrayed,
God is walking right beside you; this love has never strayed.
So let us walk together
with gratitude and grace,
Embracing a universal truth, no being can ever erase...
God is Love.
Love is God.
Fill your life with that.
Amen

June 20, 2020

Epilogue

If there is one word that I feel sums up this entire book it would be the word *Oneness*. As I really started to delve into it, I realized that I've been learning the true meaning of Oneness my whole life and continue to do so. In my youth, especially my teen years, I lived through so much yearning and loneliness to the point where when I read some of these poems, they make me cry! But I believe I was not the only one feeling this growing up. And as I've spent time especially over the last ten years talking one on one with my clients, family, and friends, I learned that they, too, often felt the same way!

In the 1990s I pretty much felt like I was living my life on default within my relationships and occupations, and that never completely satisfied this emptiness inside of me. Something felt missing. I never felt like I belonged or "fit in." I began voraciously reading as much as I could about spirituality, angels, fairies, oneness, etc. from numerous authors. I was like a sponge soaking it all in. It made me feel nourished inside and somehow connected to a "bigger picture". It was during that time I often heard my angels say to me "You have to accept the responsibility of your own gift". It took me years to figure out that they were not specifically referring to a talent or a skill; they were referring to the gift of life, and how each of us are powerful creators unto ourselves. Over time, I began to see how all is uniquely and divinely connected. Now, I believe we are not alone, never were and never will be. There is what can be seen and what cannot be seen, yet it all exists as One whether you choose to believe it or not. I named this book *My Cup is Full* not only as a title but as an affirmation to say daily and stay true to your heart and authentic self. My hope is that this book will be shared so we may begin to heal ourselves and fill that emptiness with Divine love and light! And always remember... you are loved. You are blessed. And we are one.

With Angelic Blessings,
Lisa

Use these pages to write your own inspirational thoughts.

Acknowledgments

Sean, my beloved husband and best friend, you give me wings to fly! I love you with all my heart. Thank you, my love! You are my angel! Xo

To my beautiful, talented, brave daughter, Sara. You have so much of your Meme in you! Always remember, "Mama loves you big time." xo

Dad, I love you so much. Your love for Mom is so inspiring to all. I have always said you were from another planet because you are an incredible person! Lucky me! Xo

Lastly, to some incredibly supportive earth angels that I love— Erika Jean Fournier-Duarte, Linda Biron, Jane Murphy, Annie Bienkiewicz Ducharme, Patty Stamp, Rachel Fox, and Christina Rondeau. Enormous octopus hugs!

Thank you for everything!

Peace

www.ingramcontent.com/pod-product-compliance
Lightning Source LLC
Chambersburg PA
CBHW060054100426
42742CB00014B/2830